# WANDERLAND

Drawings by EMMANUEL PIERRE

Text by BRUNO GAUDICHON

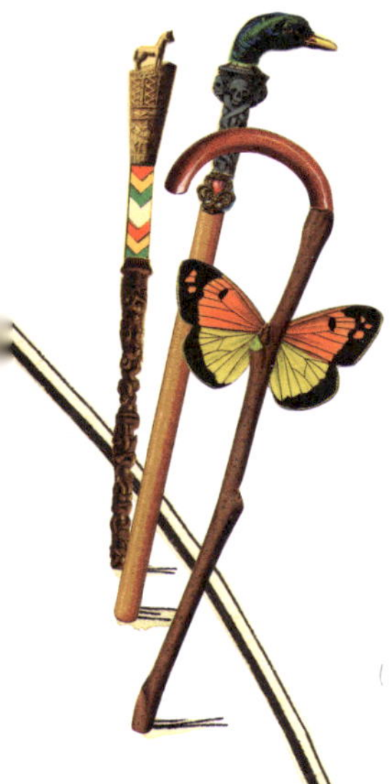



*ACTES SUD | HERMÈS*

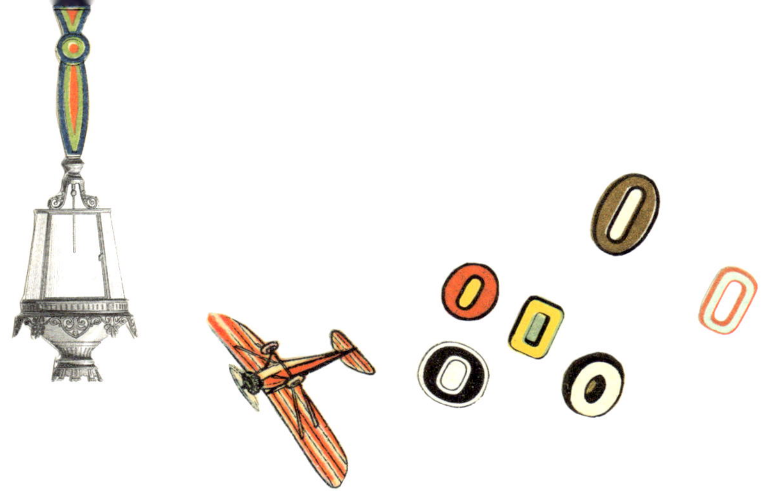

Flânerie is second nature to Hermès. In fact, it is what we are all about. Everything in this industrious house arises from, and encourages, this art of visual gleaning. Our decorative objects, our window displays, even the stores themselves are conceived to inspire this very Parisian practice that seems not about lost time but time regained. For let us not be fooled: the flâneur's leisureliness is also a state of alertness. Heightened, the senses all play their part in this unhasty state: sight, hearing and smell above all, but touch and taste are not far behind. Guided by instinct, the flâneur is on the lookout for the fleeting, decisive moment, ready to seize it in a dashing refutation of his apparent nonchalance. In that sense, flânerie is like hunting in its mixture of slowness and vivacity. The unforeseen and the unknown are the flâneur's great prey, his favoured game.

Here I think of my great grandfather, Émile Hermès, a visionary entrepreneur, who had those twin talents of impenitent flâneur and compulsive collector. Even today, the objects that caught his fancy are a true goldmine of inspiration for all our métiers. Better than anyone else, the flâneur spots the novel in the humdrum, the unseen in the déjà vu, the faraway in the local, and the visible in the invisible. Flânerie can thus be seen as a practice of metamorphosis: the metamorphosis of constrained, alienated time into free time, time for the self. A metamorphosis of familiar space into a terra incognita, an adventure playground. And, ultimately, a metamorphosis of our relation to ourselves, to others and to the world. Flânerie is, at heart, a poetic practice, a creative practice. That is why so many artists, whether poets, illustrators, painters or photographers, are inveterate flâneurs. Clearly, then, the flâneur is no idler, just as the dreamer is anything but empty-headed.

PIERRE-ALEXIS DUMAS

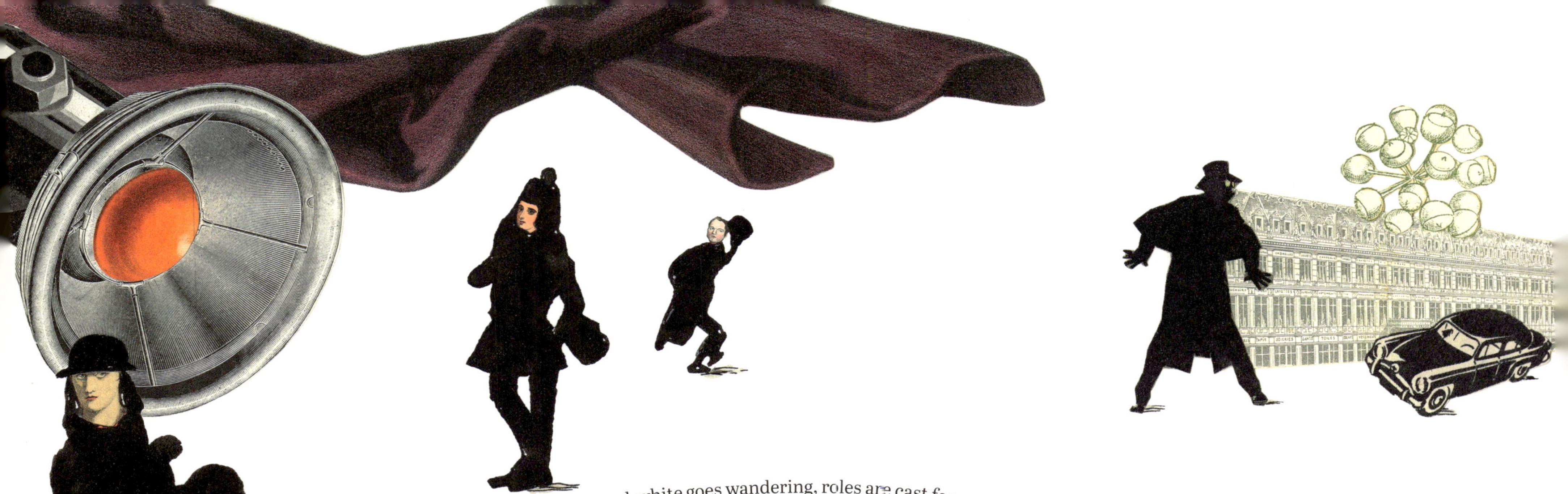

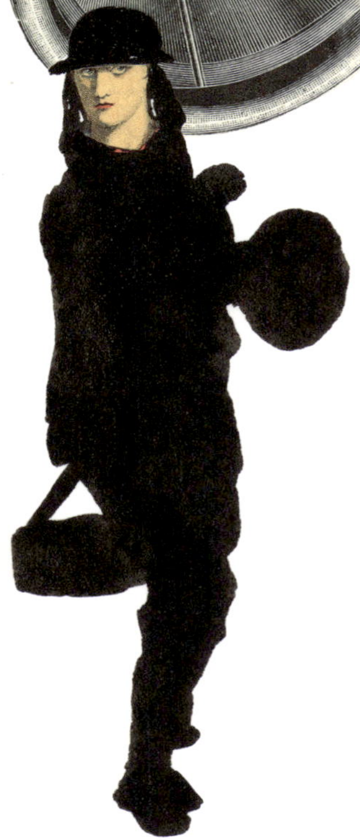

On the screen of where a script for black-and-white goes wandering, roles are cast for nomadic dreamers electrified by the pleasure of a magnetic race to Paris. Here

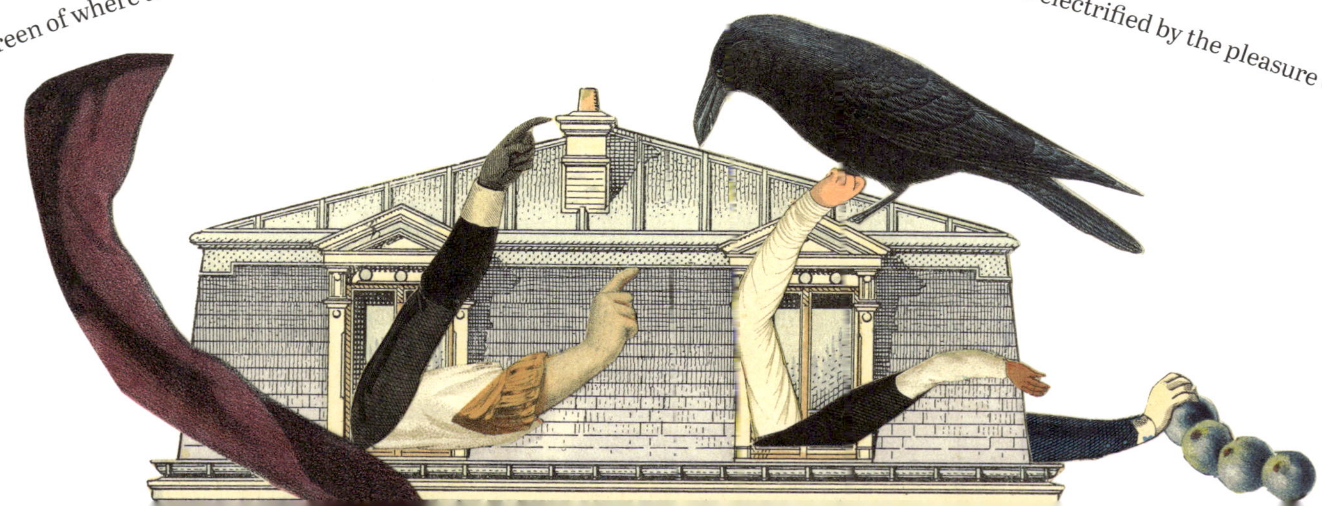

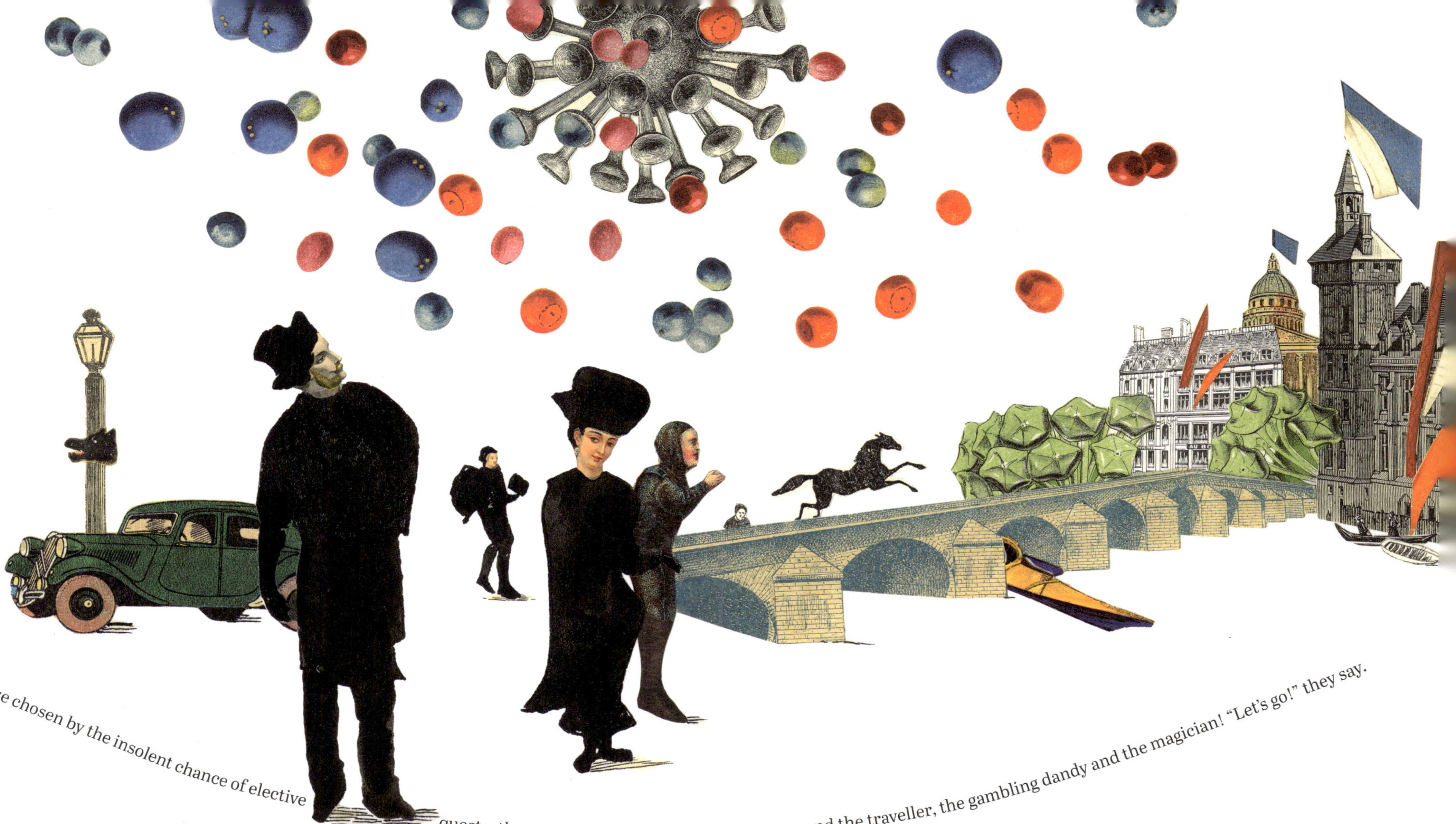

those chosen by the insolent chance of elective quests, the artist and the writer, the horseman and the traveller, the gambling dandy and the magician! “Let’s go!” they say.

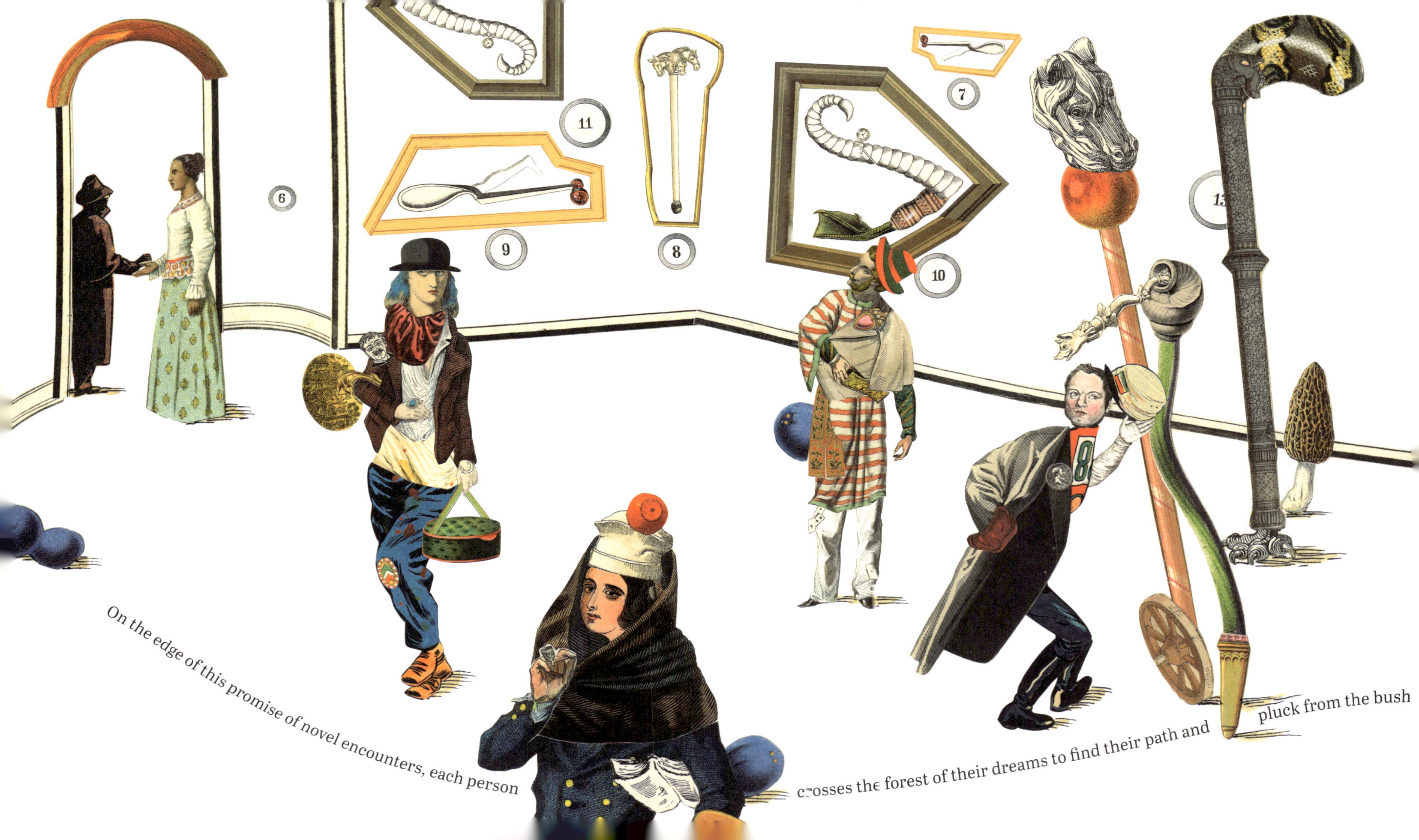


On the edge of this promise of novel encounters, each person crosses the forest of their dreams to find their path and pluck from the bush

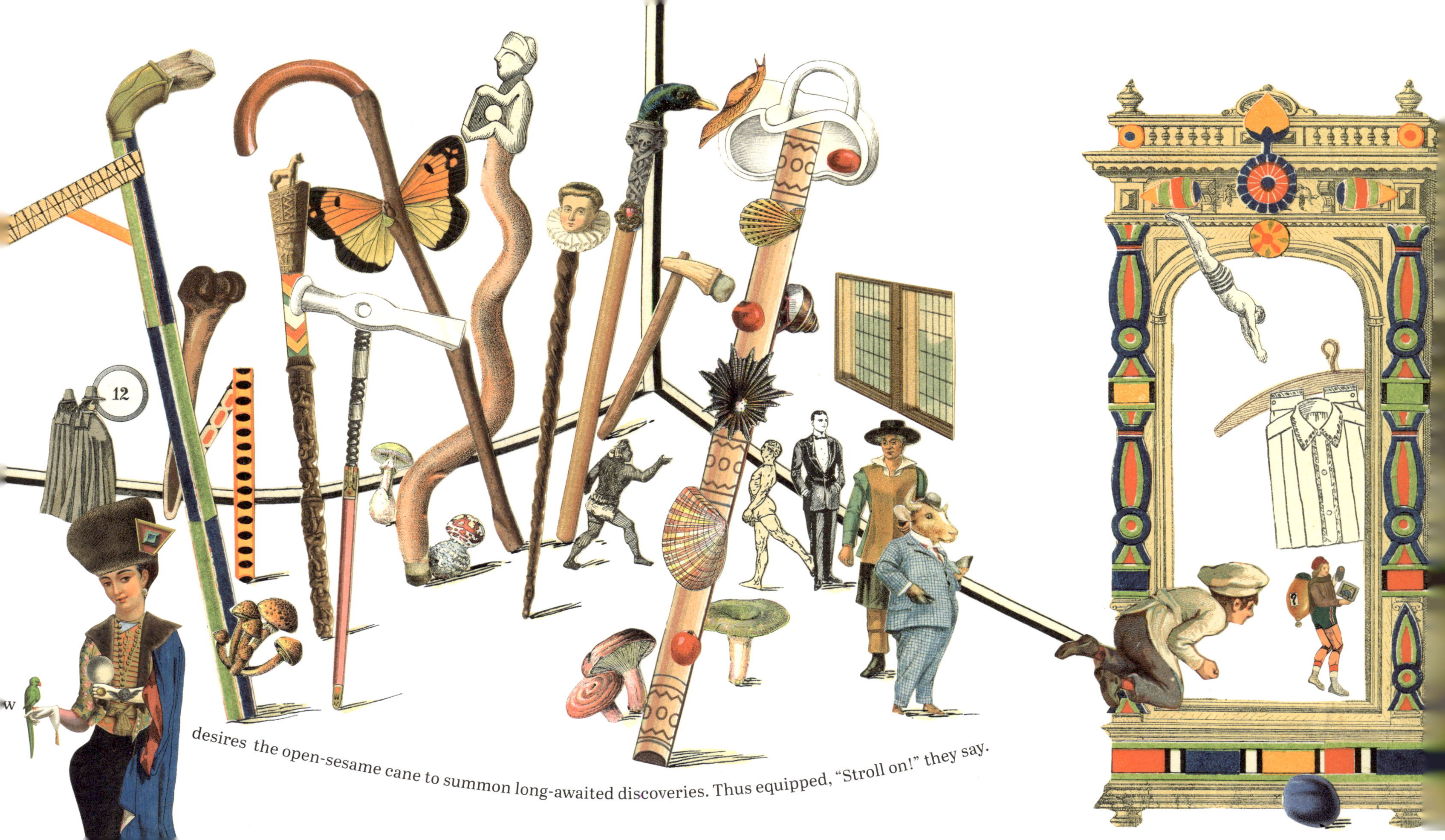


w

desires the open-sesame cane to summon long-awaited discoveries. Thus equipped, “Stroll on!” they say.

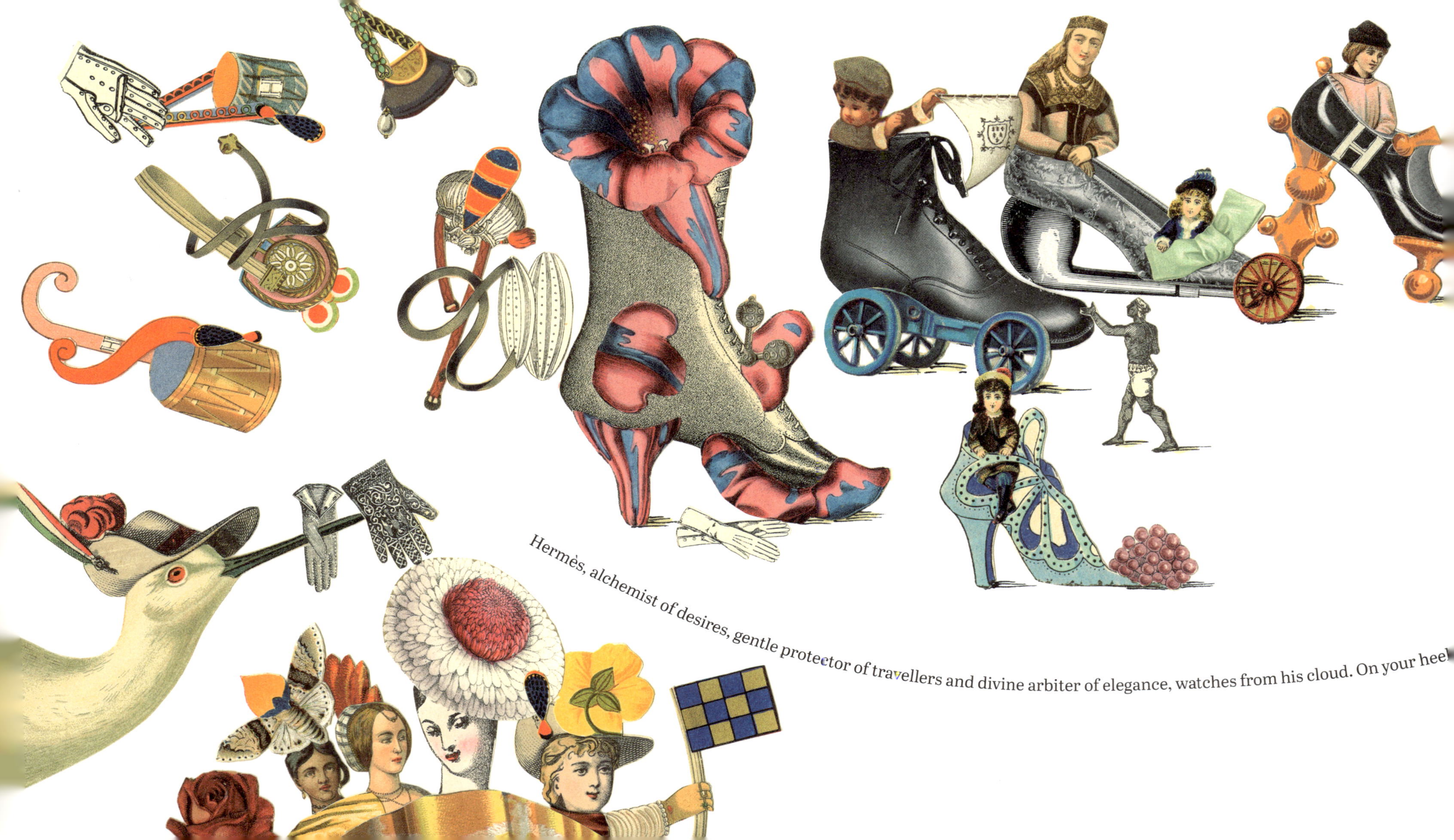

Hermès, alchemist of desires, gentle protector of travellers and divine arbiter of elegance, watches from his cloud. On your heel

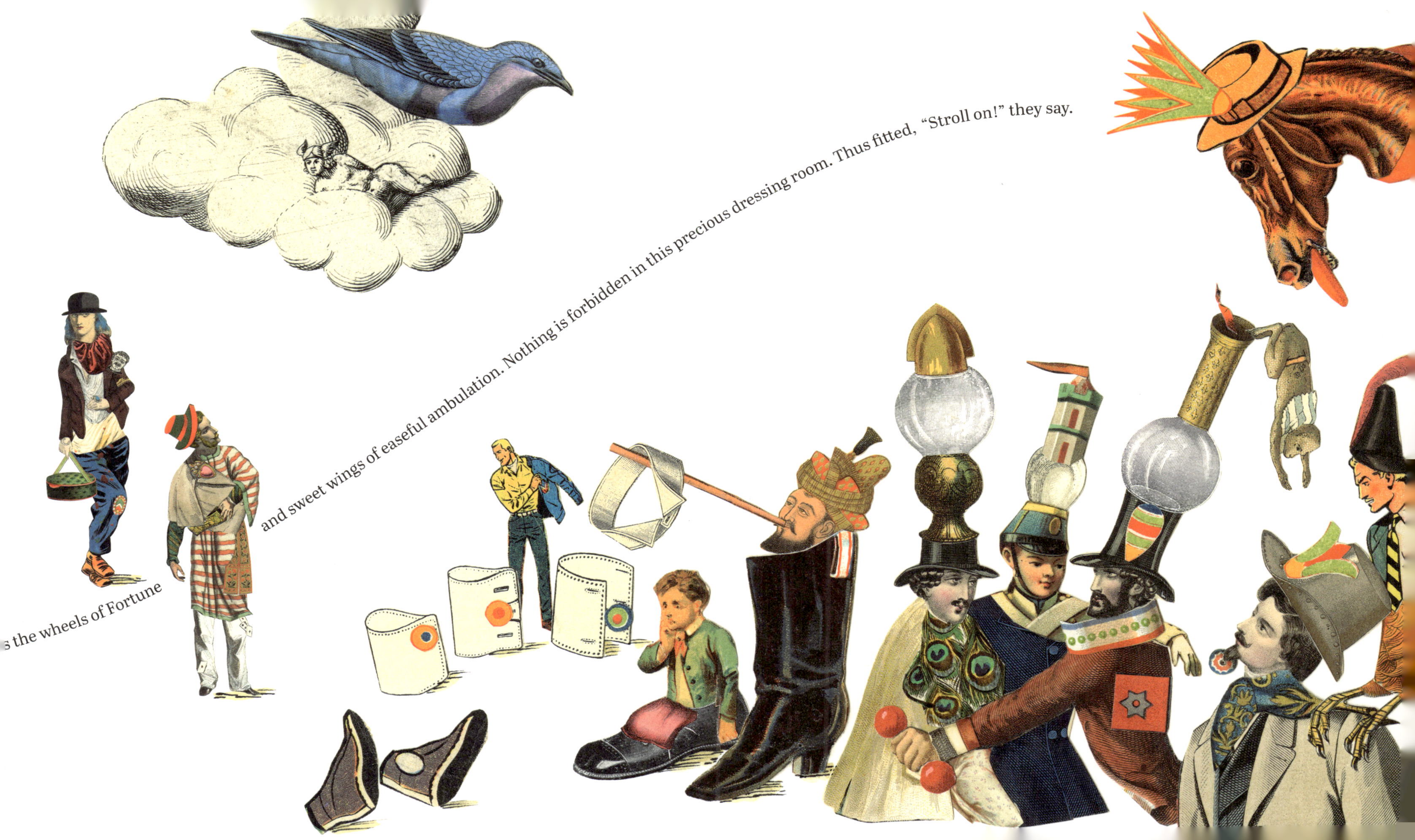

s the wheels of Fortune

and sweet wings of easeful ambulation. Nothing is forbidden in this precious dressing room. Thus fitted, “Stroll on!” they say.

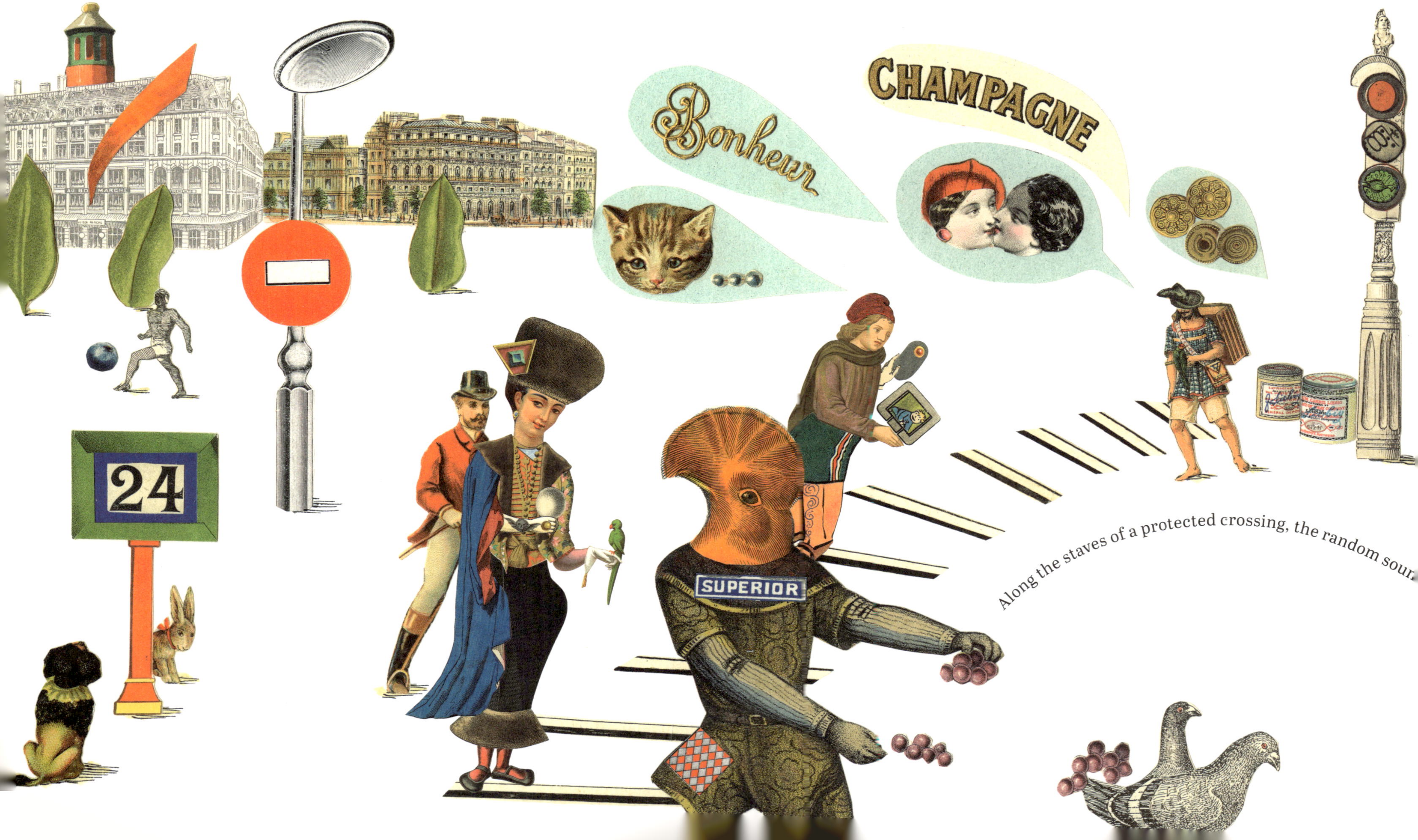


Along the staves of a protected crossing, the random sour

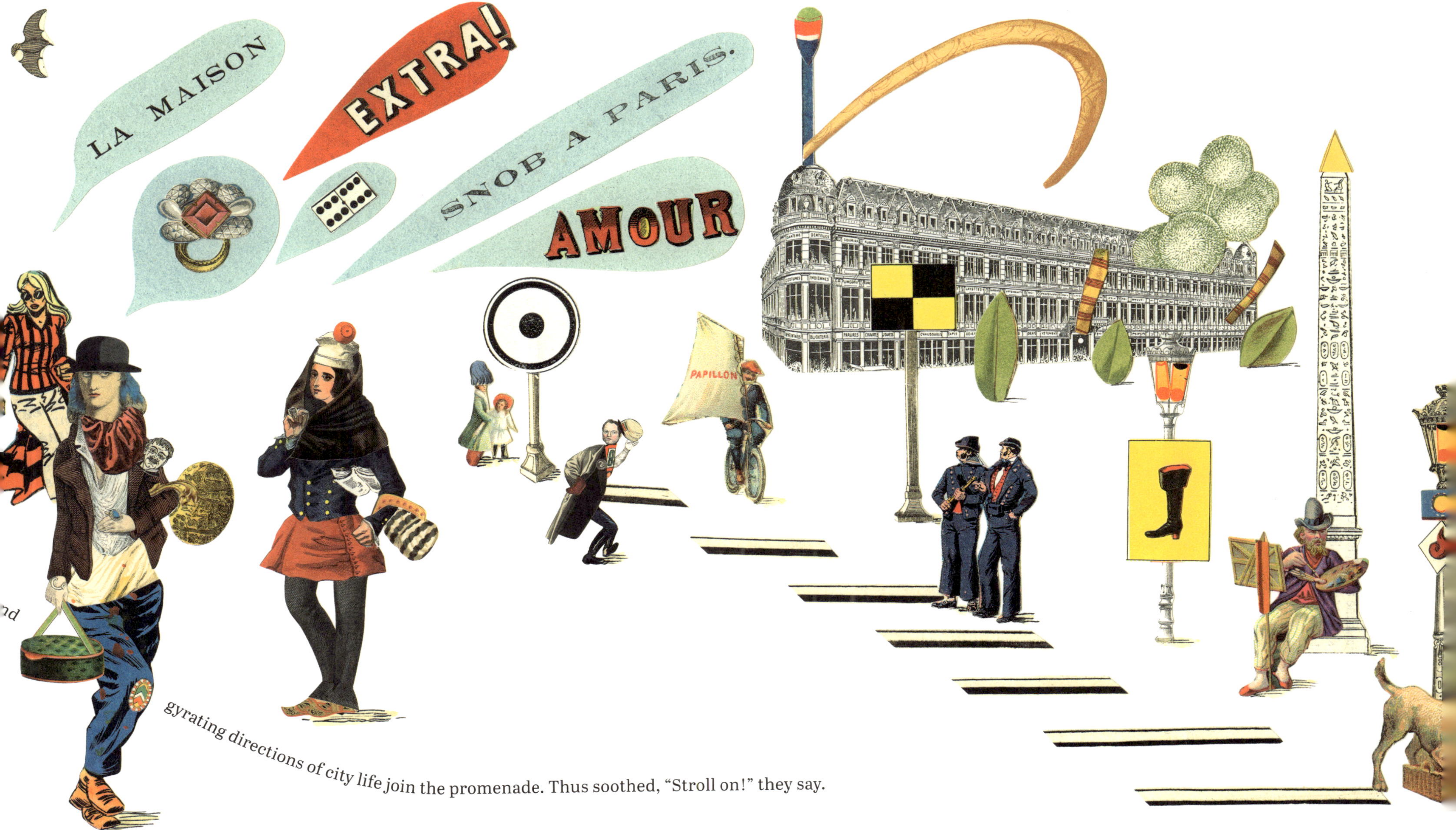


nd

gyrating directions of city life join the promenade. Thus soothed, “Stroll on!” they say.

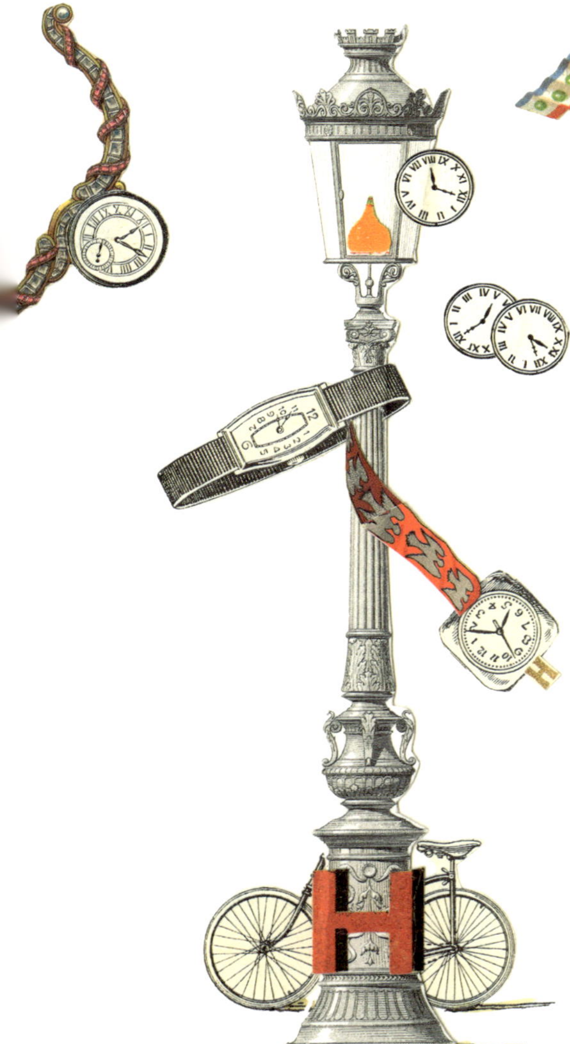

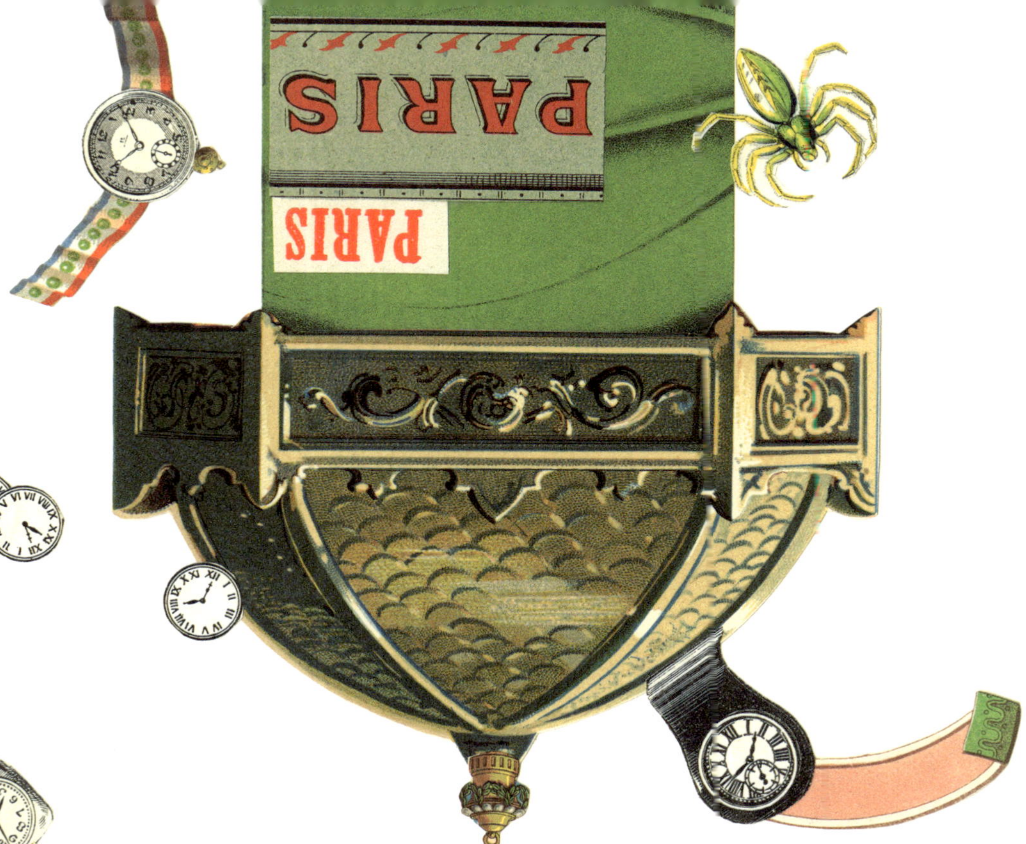


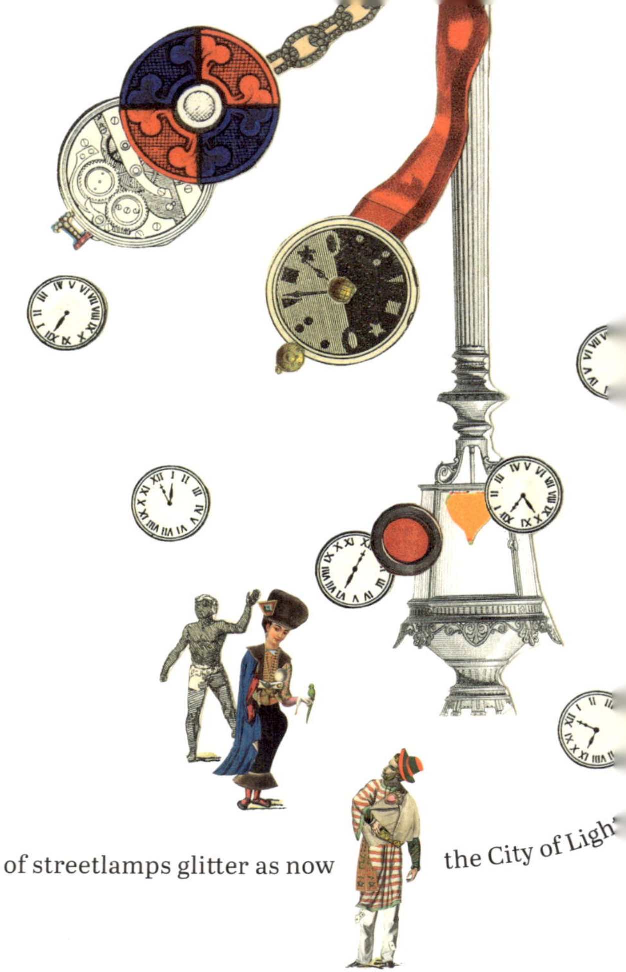

Topsy-turvy, the alluring images of the Morris columns and glass orbs of streetlamps glitter as now the City of Ligh

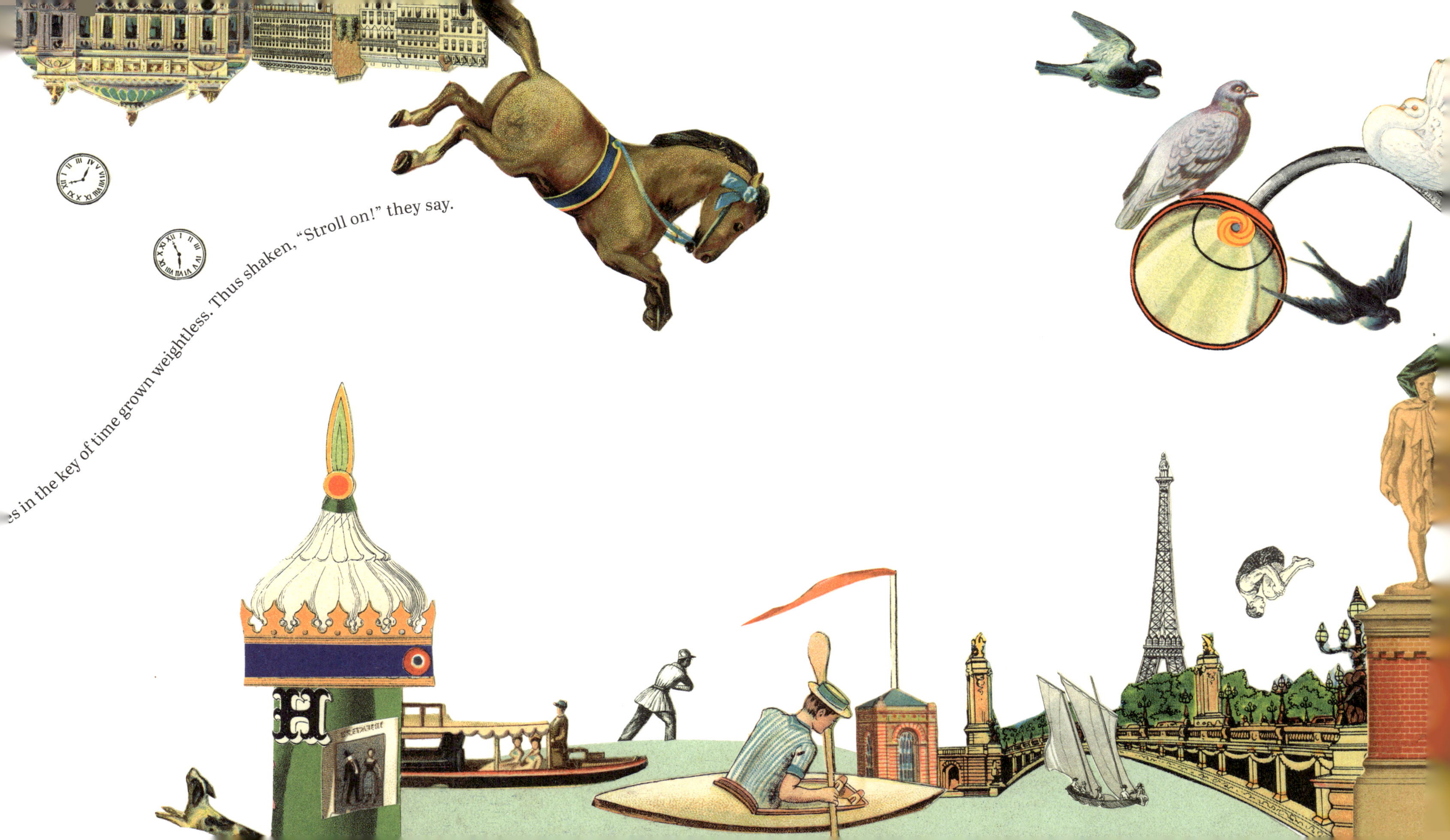

es in the key of time grown weightless. Thus shaken, “Stroll on!” they say.

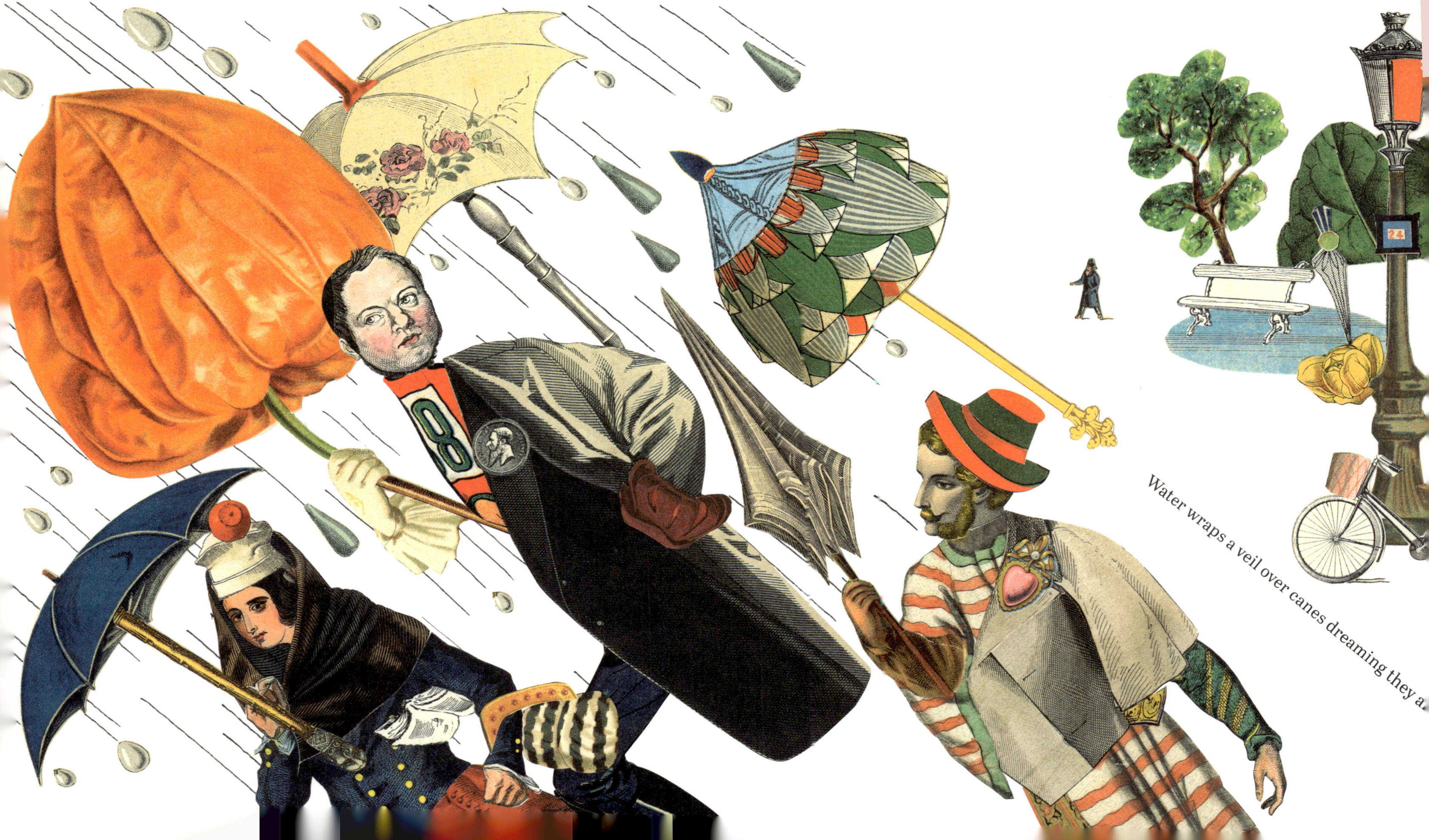

Water wraps a veil over canes dreaming they a

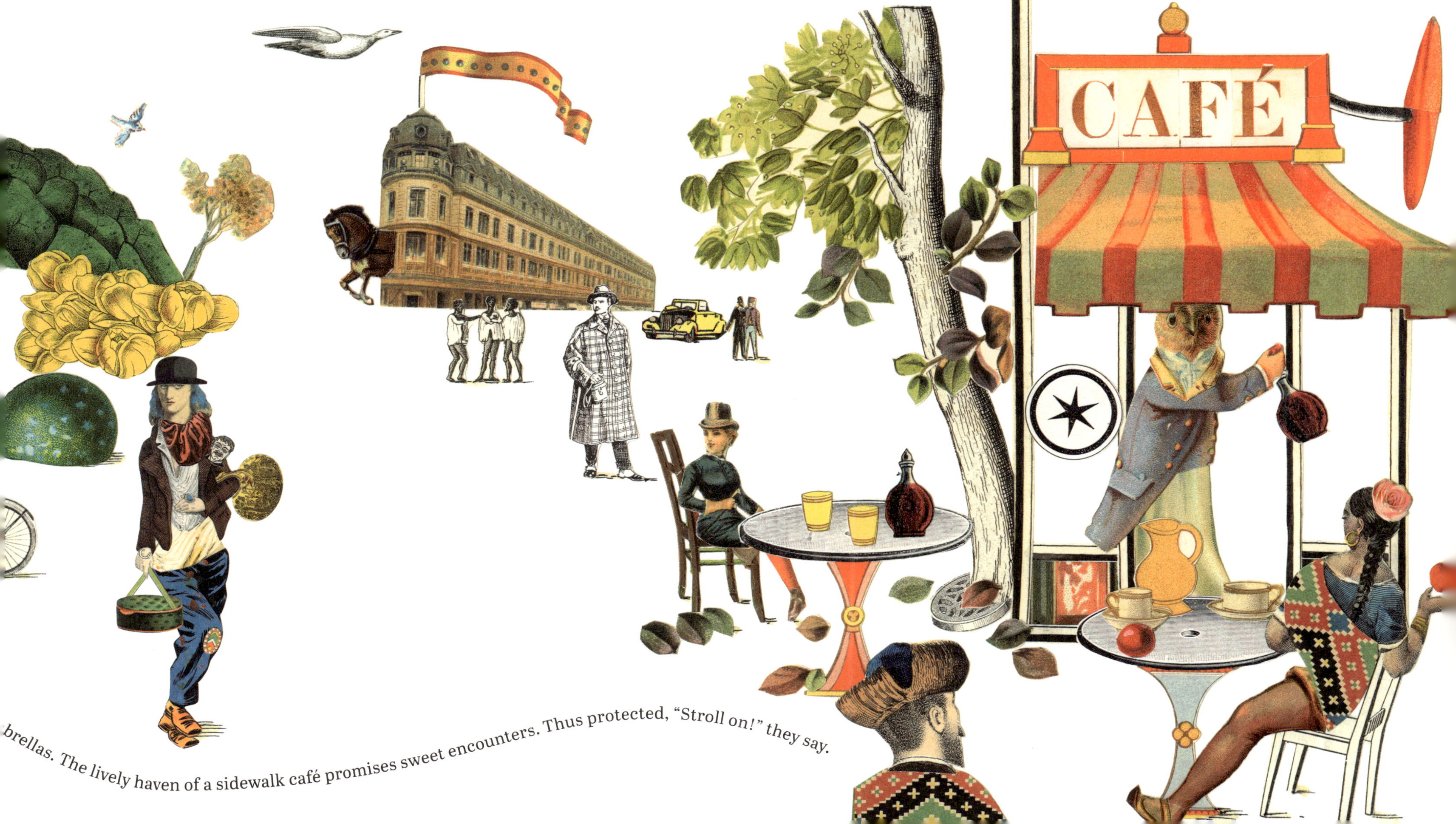


brellas. The lively haven of a sidewalk café promises sweet encounters. Thus protected, “Stroll on!” they say.

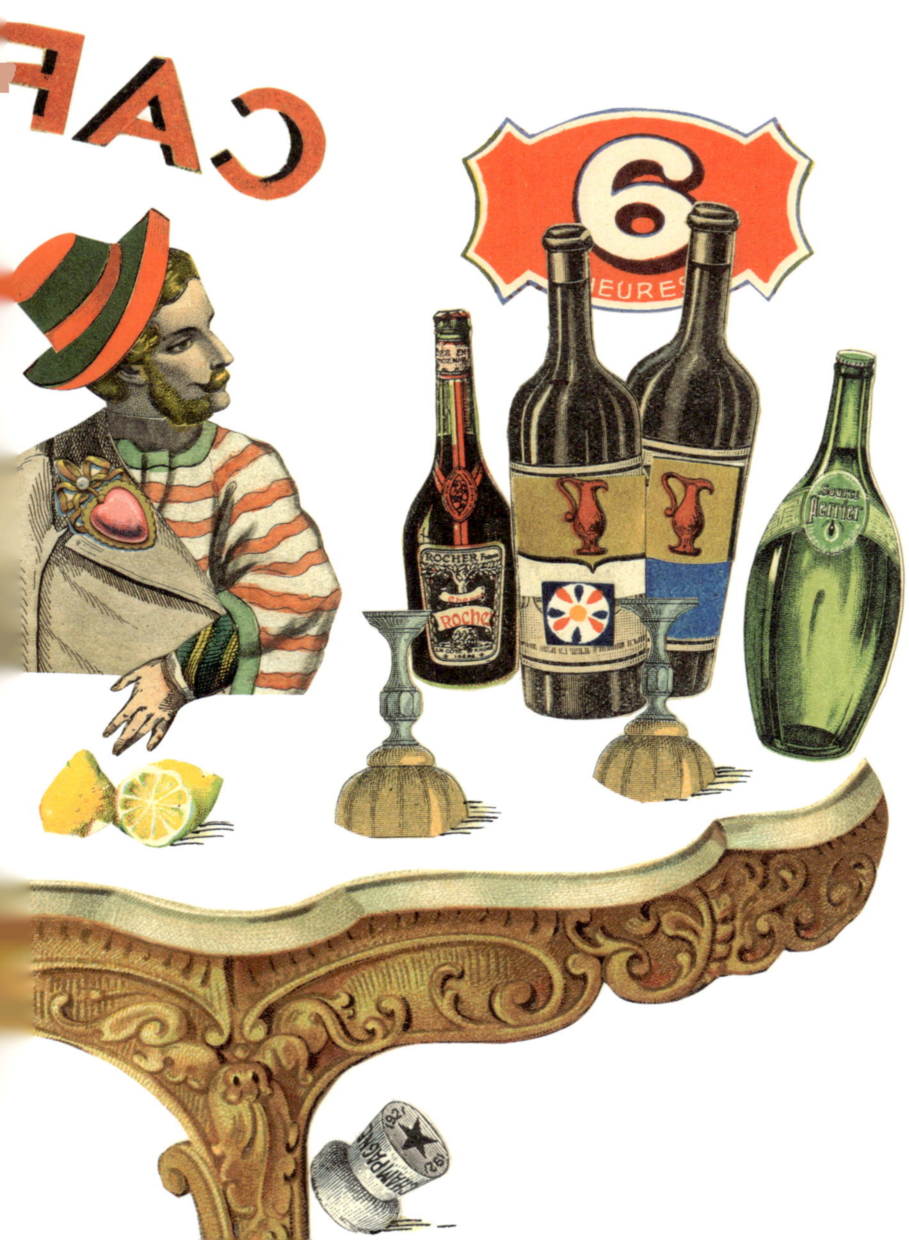


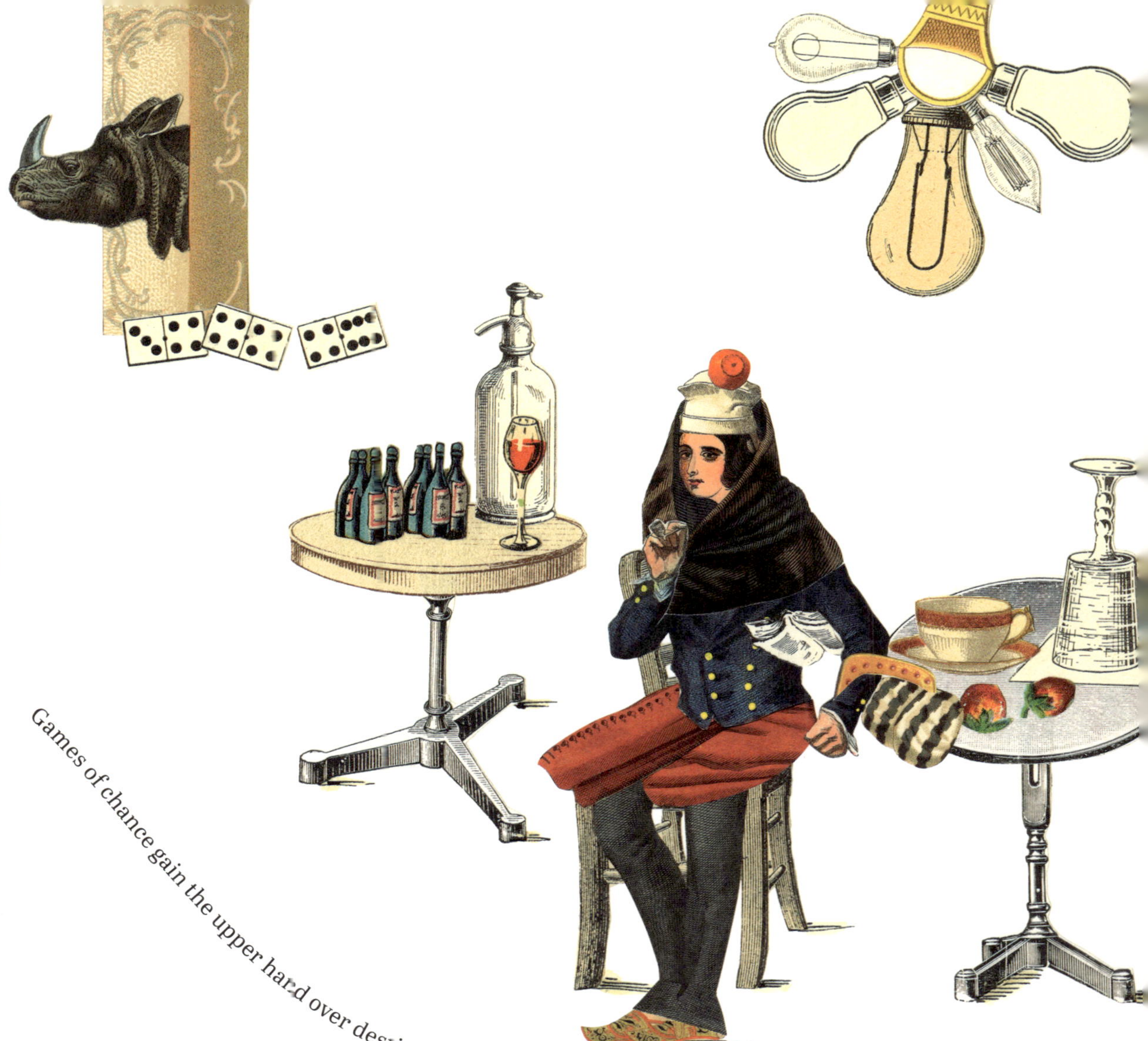

Games of chance gain the upper hard over destiny in the golden glow of burning acetylene lamps. In the heady confusi

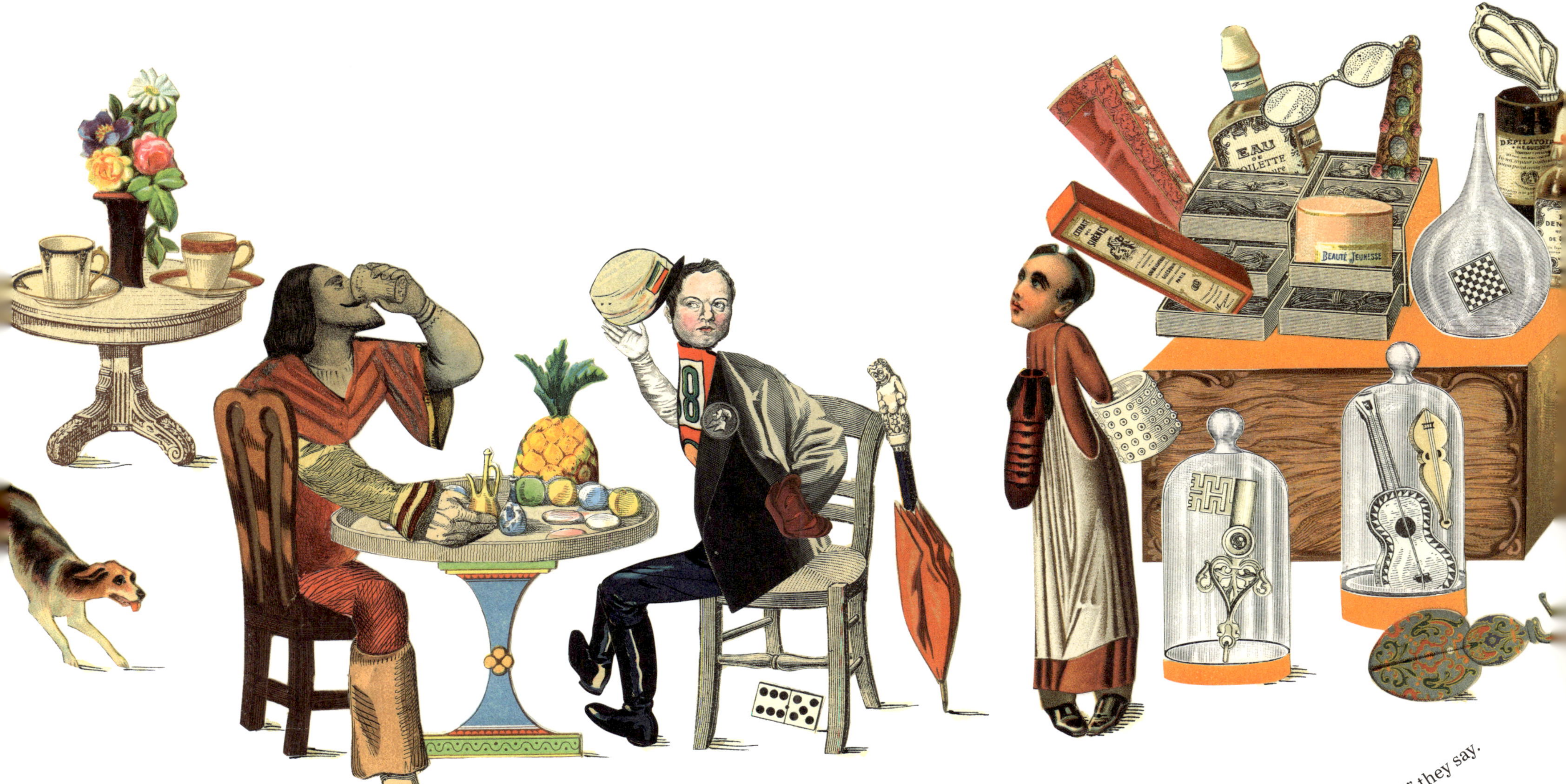


rossed gazes, the remains of a toothsome stopover linger on the cool of the marble and in the crystalline cages of bottles. Thus remiss, “Stroll on!” they say.

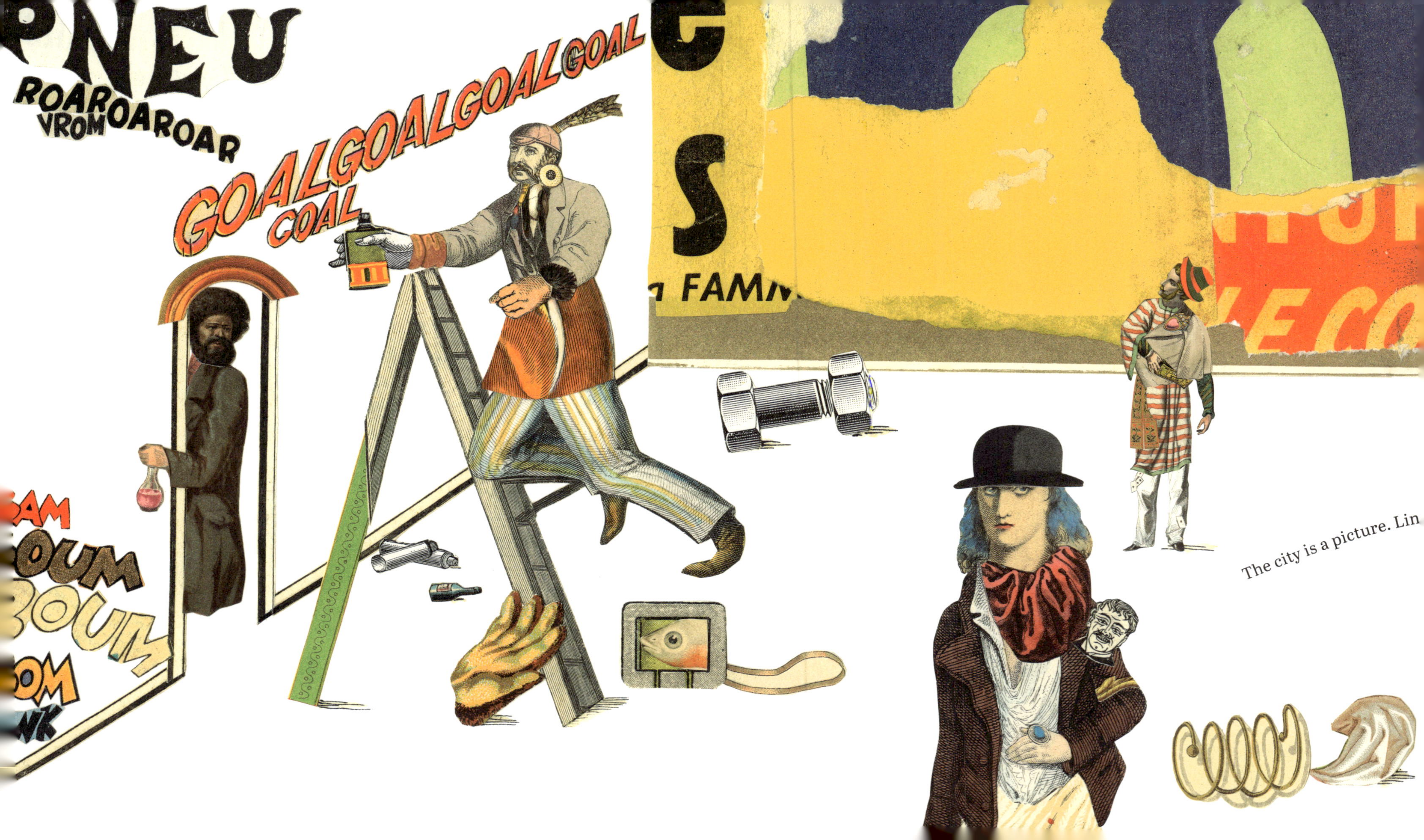


The city is a picture. Lin

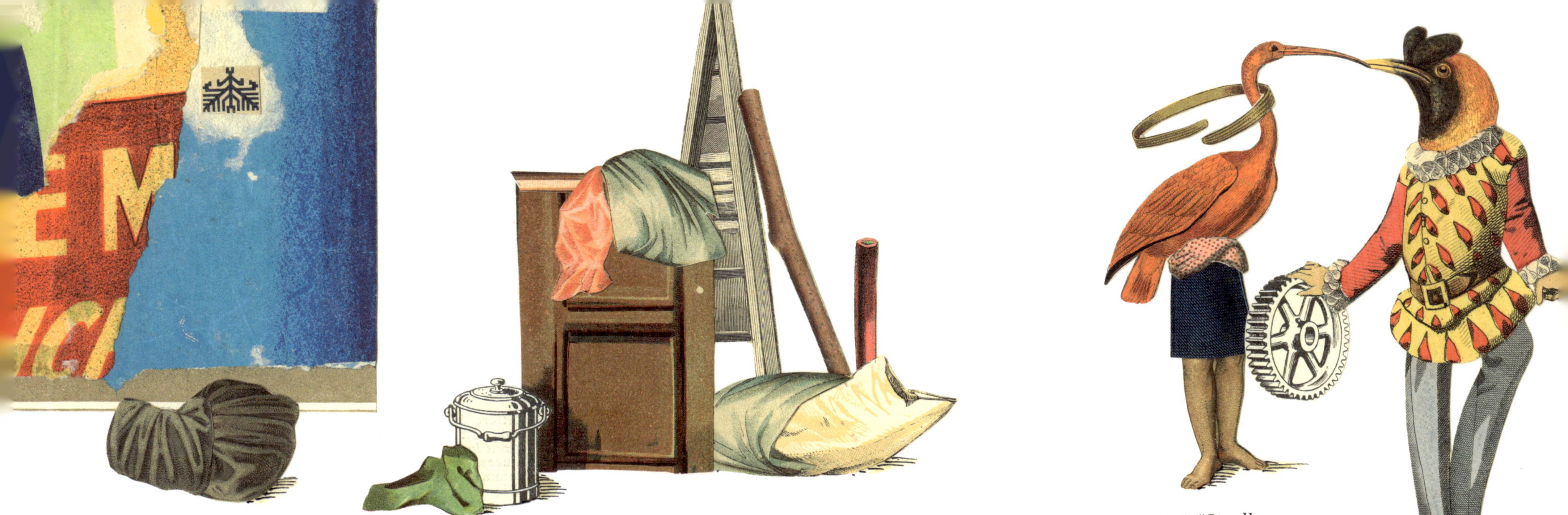

lour and the unruly skins of posters all bring art into the street. The artist's eye nestles in the fleeting pixels of a graphic tablet. Thus dazzled, "Stroll on!" they say.

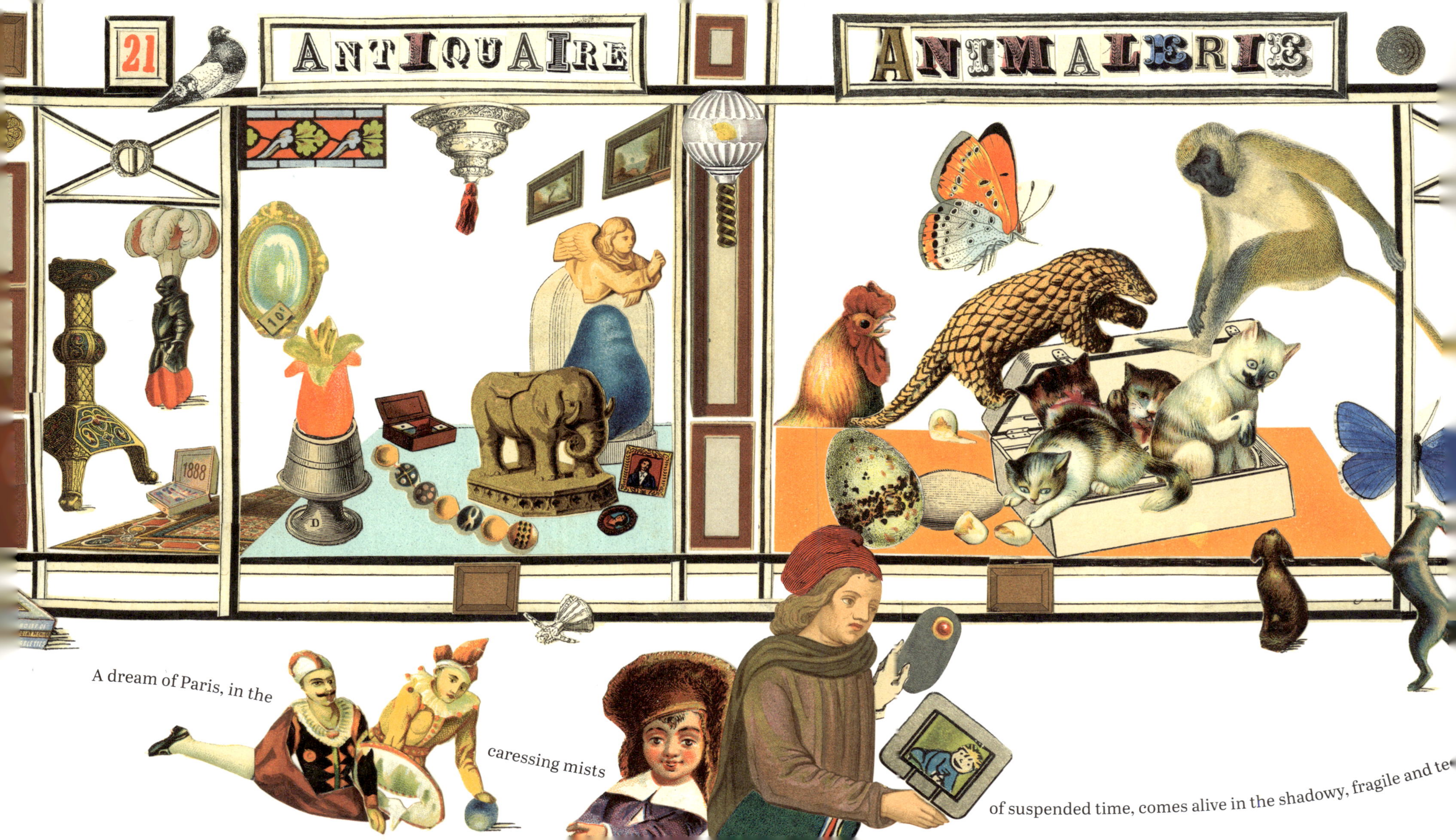


A dream of Paris, in the caressing mists of suspended time, comes alive in the shadowy, fragile and te

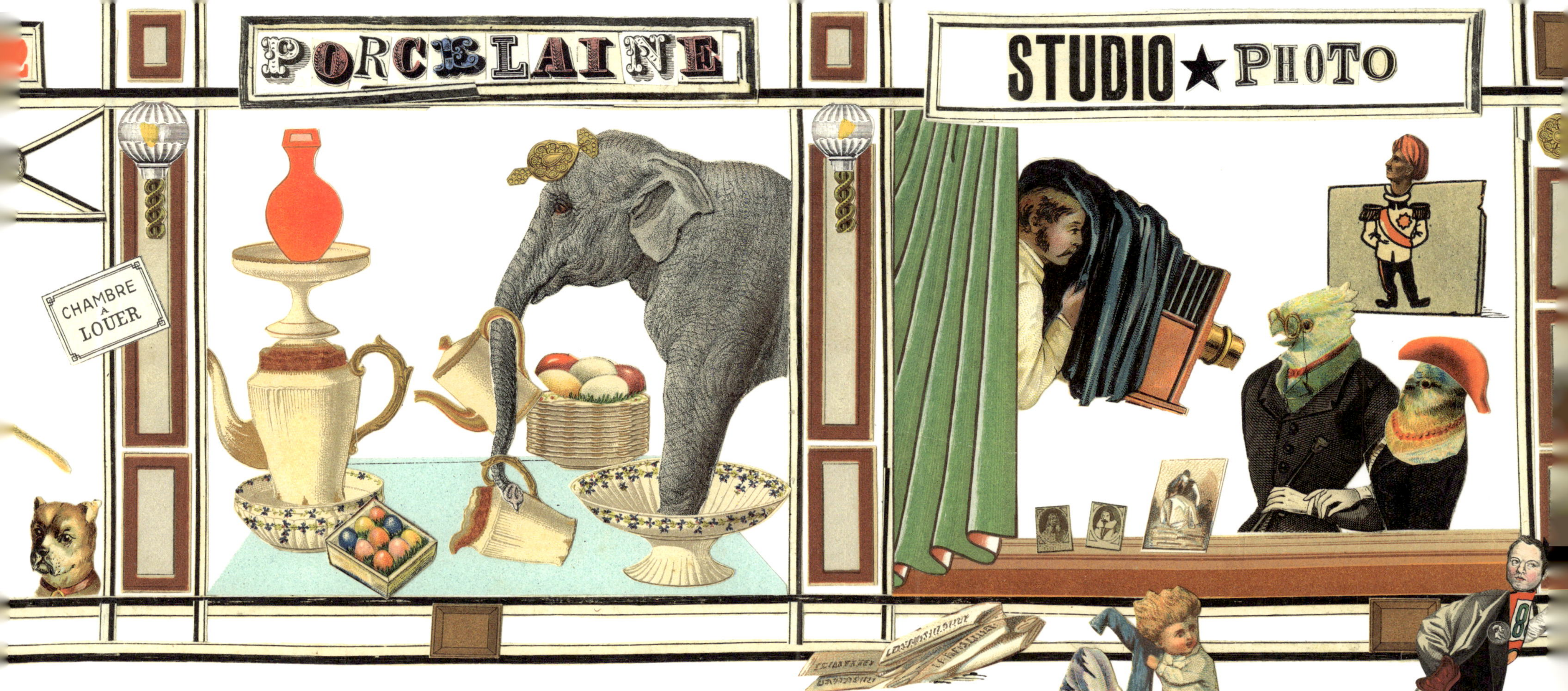


, magic of arcades. Inside-outside, the flâneur’s steps stray amidst the strange inventory of stalls of other places, other times, life and images. Thus seduced, “Stroll on!” they say.

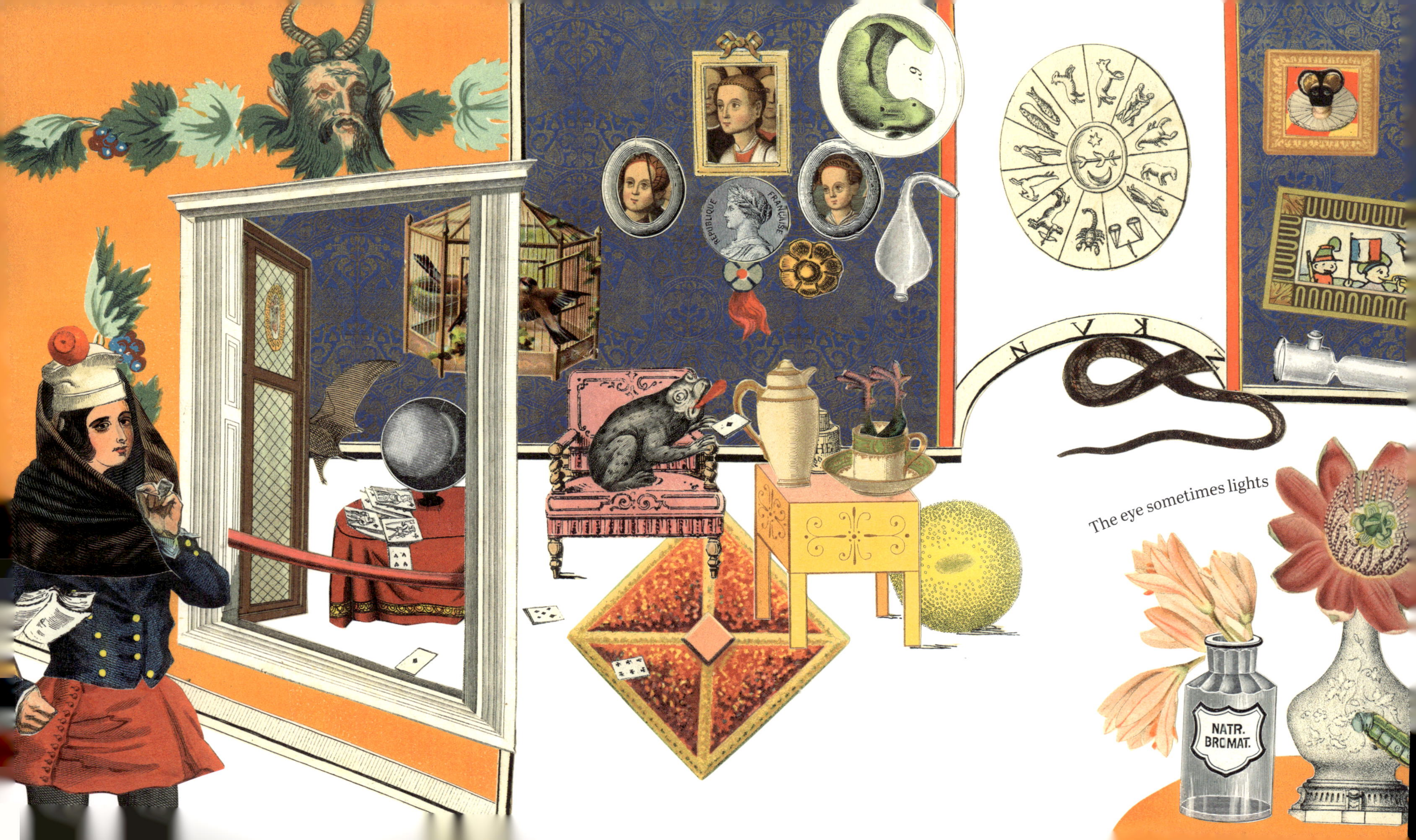


The eye sometimes lights

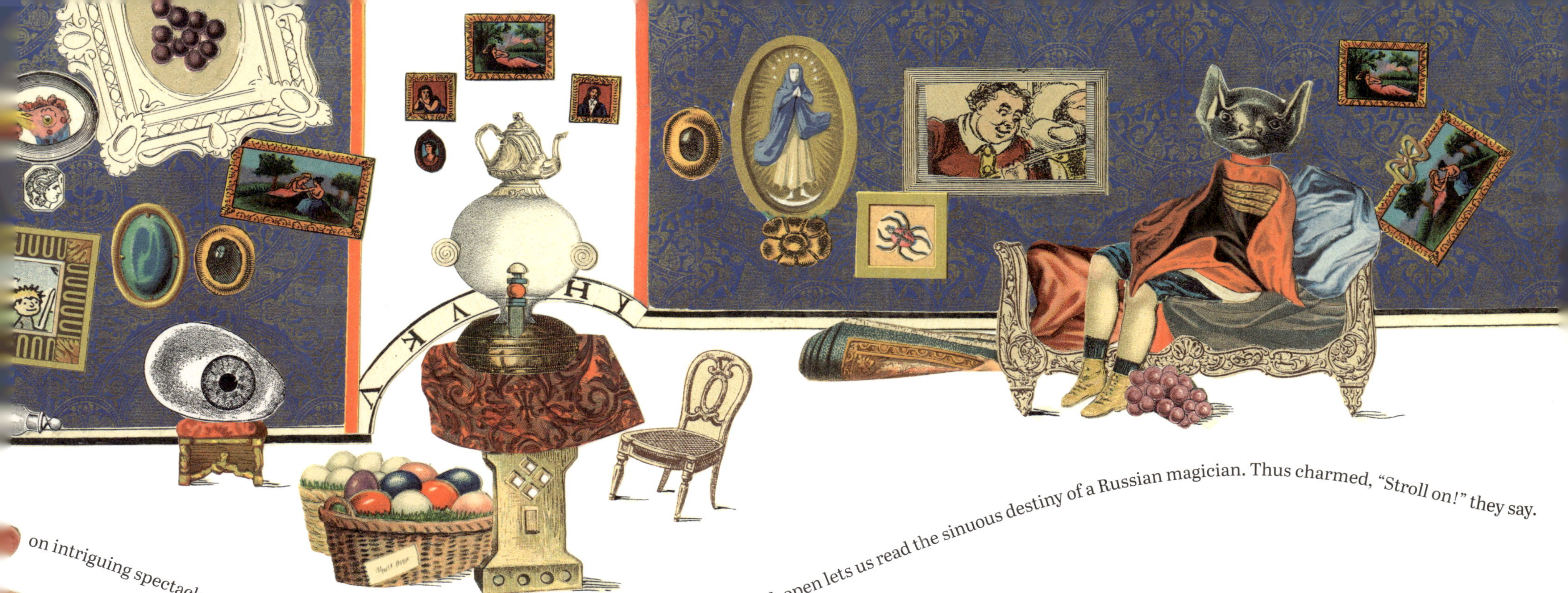

on intriguing spectacles. Random upshots of these inspiring intrusions, the charm of a lodge left open lets us read the sinuous destiny of a Russian magician. Thus charmed, “Stroll on!” they say.

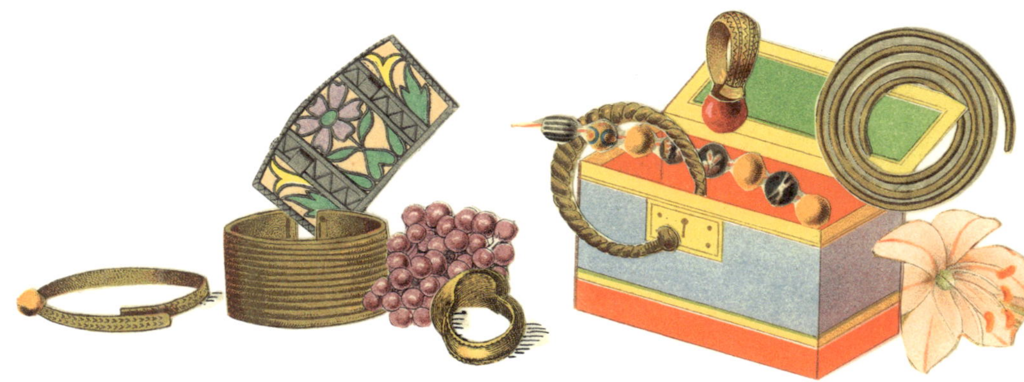

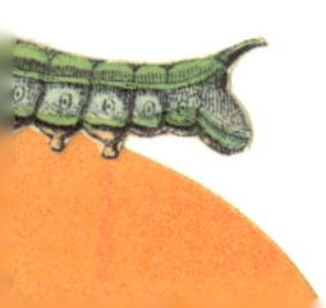

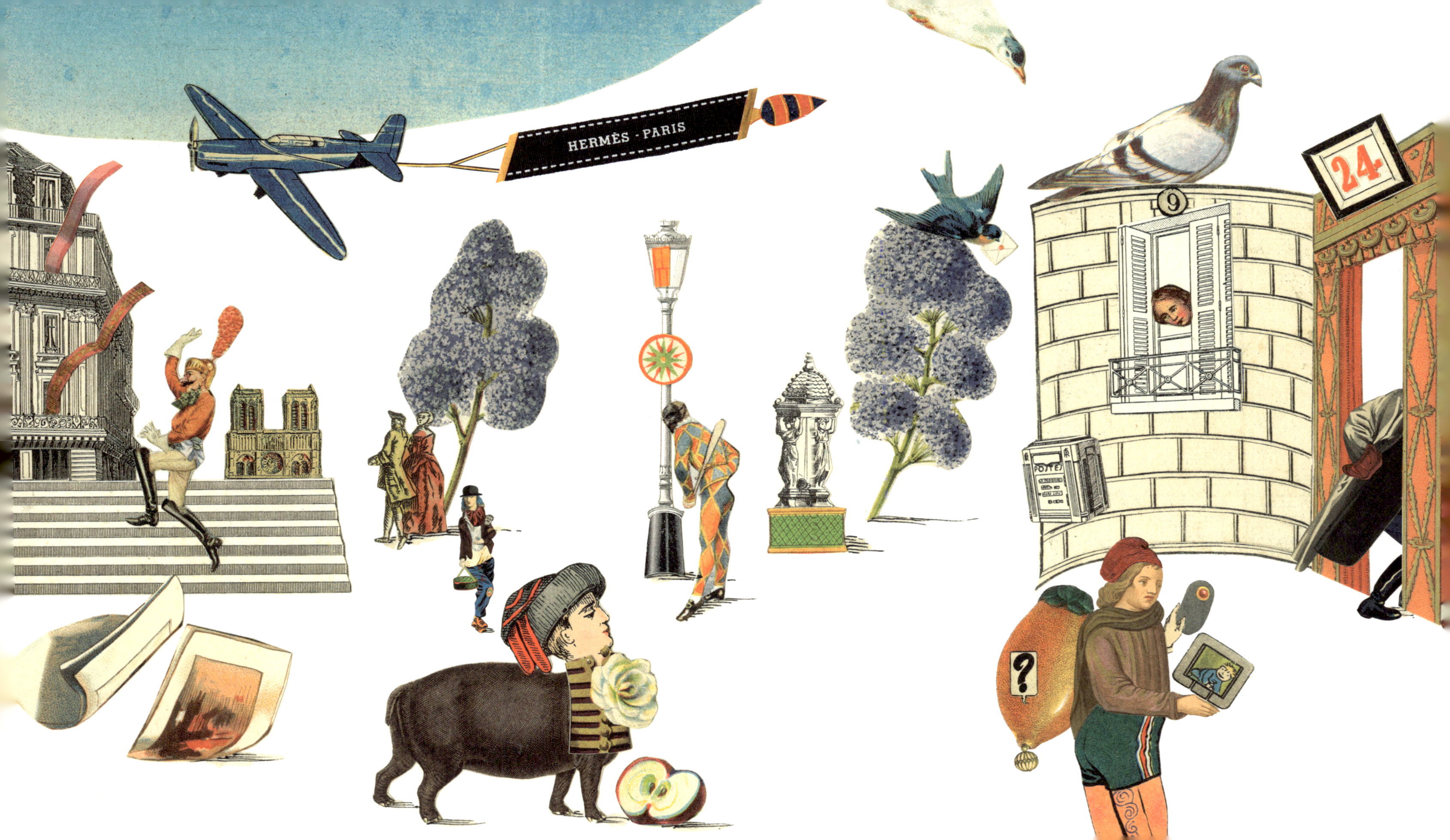
HERMÈS · PARIS
24
9
POSTES
?

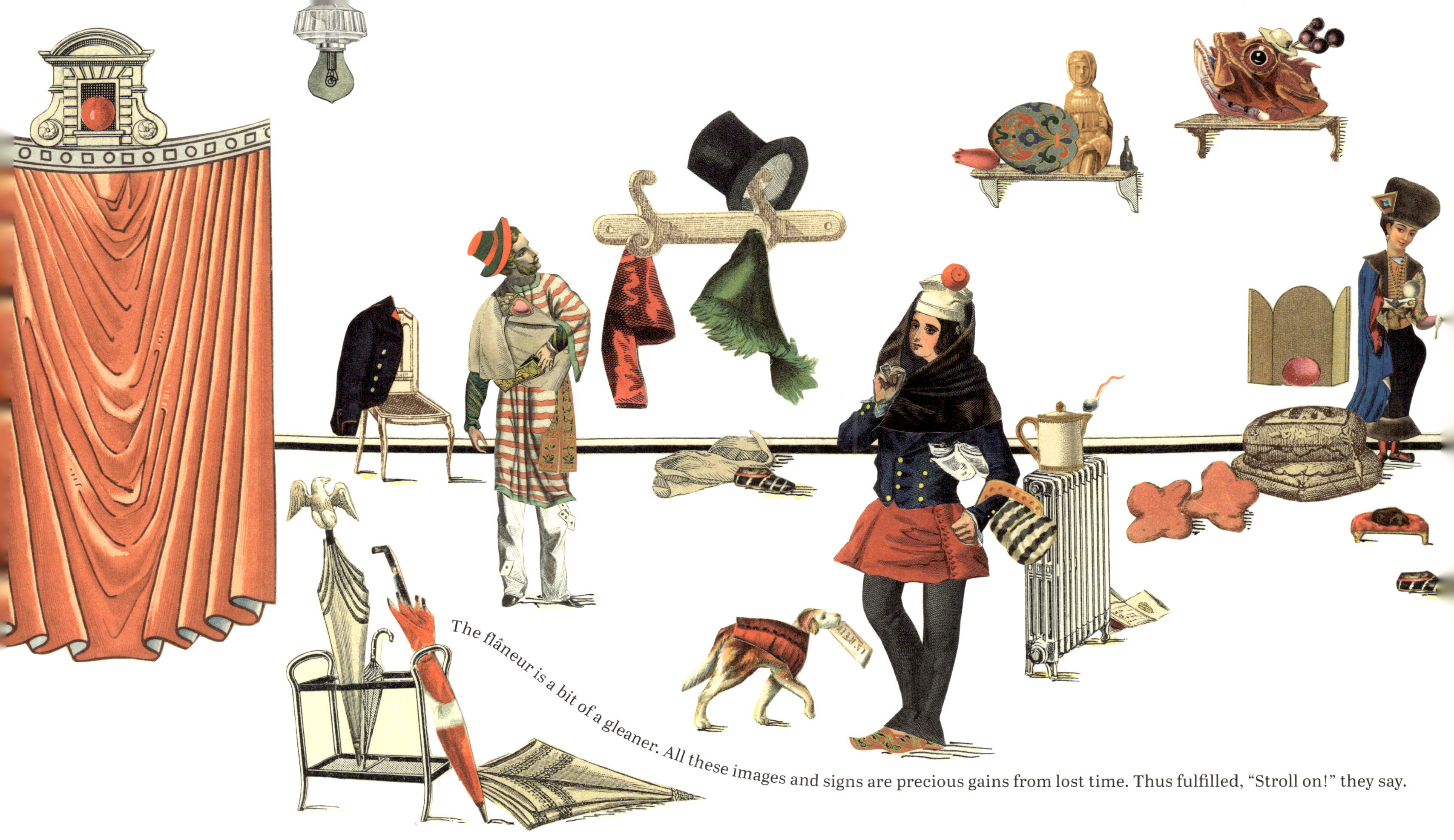

The flâneur is a bit of a gleaner. All these images and signs are precious gains from lost time. Thus fulfilled, “Stroll on!” they say.

ACKNOWLEDGEMENTS

Pierre-Alexis Dumas, Artistic Director of Hermès, would like to thank all those who, through their talent and perseverance, made the exhibition *Wanderland* possible, particularly Bruno Gaudichon, who curated it, and Hubert le Gall, who designed it. He is also grateful to Emmanuel Pierre, who marvellously illustrated this book inspired by the exhibition, and to publishers Actes Sud, especially Anne-Sylvie Bameule and Raphaëlle Pinoncély.



Hermès editorial coordination: Pierre-Alexis Dumas,
Adrien Barrot, Cosima Balsan *assisted by* Charlotte Lévy
Actes Sud editorial coordination: Anne-Sylvie Bameule
Graphic design: Raphaëlle Pinoncély
Translation: Charles Penwarden
Proofreading: Bronwyn Mahoney
Production: Géraldine Lay
Photoengraving: Quatcoul, France

This book was printed in February 2015
by Grafiche AZ, Italy, for the publisher Actes Sud,
Le Méjan, Place Nina-Berberova, 13200 Arles.


ISBN 978-2-330-04913-3
Legal deposit 1st edition: April 2015
www.actes-sud.fr

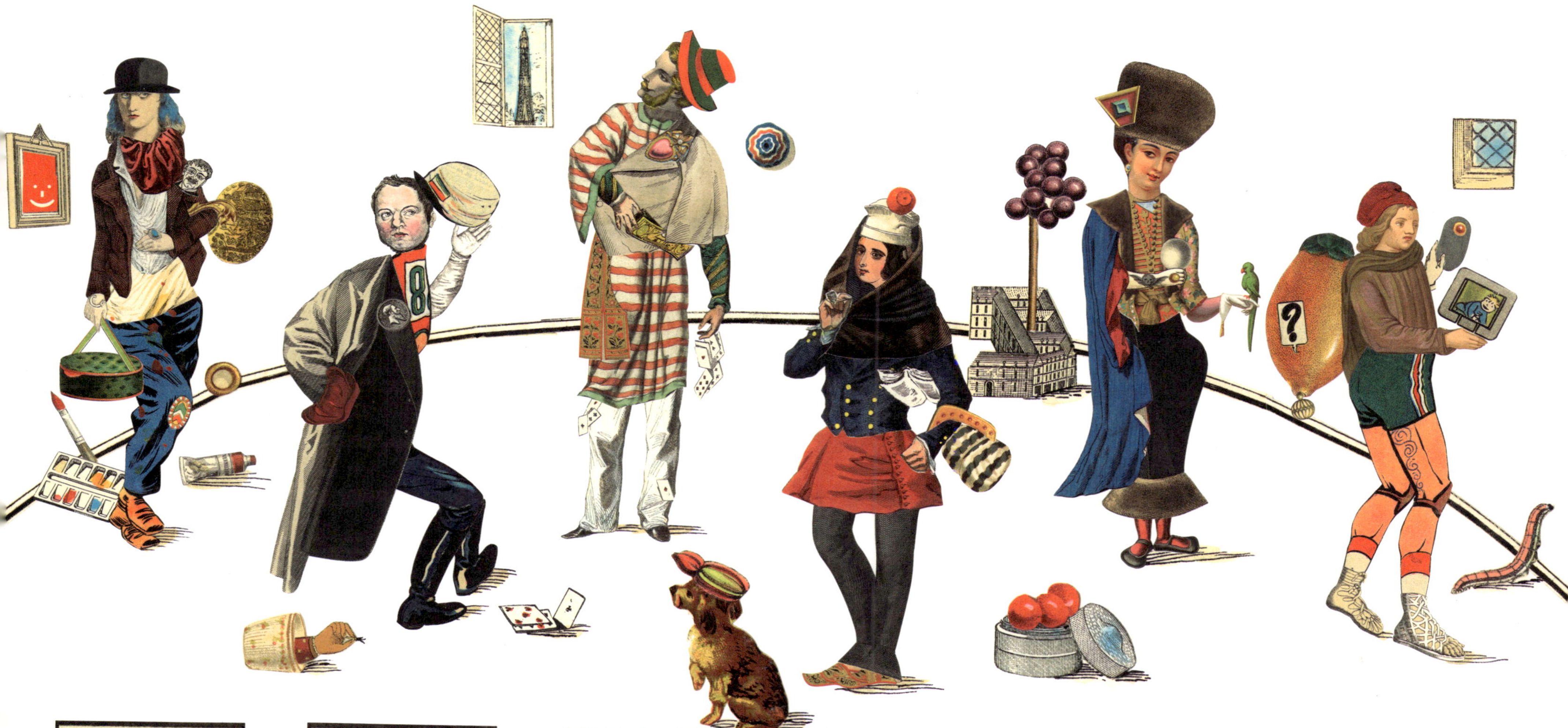

The artist | The horseman | The gambling dandy | The writer | The magician | The traveller